Original title:
The Banana Split Dream

Copyright © 2025 Creative Arts Management OÜ
All rights reserved.

Author: Julian Montgomery
ISBN HARDBACK: 978-1-80586-470-7
ISBN PAPERBACK: 978-1-80586-942-9

Enchanted Nights in a Sweet Retreat

In the land where sprinkles rain,
Chocolate rivers flow like champagne,
Sundaes dance with cherry hats,
While jellybeans jump on playful mats.

Waffle cones meet the giant scoops,
Whipped cream swirls in happy loops,
Banana boats sail on minty seas,
With laughter echoing through the trees.

Peanut butter clouds float overhead,
Cupcake mountains where dreams are fed,
Cotton candy spins in a dizzy whirl,
As gummy bears do a silly twirl.

Magic lingers in the warm night air,
Cupfuls of joy beyond compare,
Delightful giggles from every treat,
In this wonderland, oh so sweet!

Summertime Wishes in Every Bite

Underneath the bright sun's glow,
Frozen dreams begin to flow,
Slices of joy on colorful plates,
A dessert feast that elates.

Ice cream slides down sugar hills,
Each afternoon, the laughter spills,
Cone-wielding kiddos march in line,
With sticky hands and smiles that shine.

Chocolate fudge makes the best disguise,
As spry squirrels sneak with hungry eyes,
They plot and plan for a creamy taste,
In this sugary race, there's no time to waste.

Joyful crunch in every spoon,
Chasing flavors beneath the moon,
With every bite, a wish is made,
In this summer feast, fun won't fade!

Chilled Bliss and Crunchy Whirls

In a bowl of fun, we dive so deep,
With scoops that laugh and flavors that leap.
Nuts are prancing, whipped cream does twirl,
Chilled bliss awaits in a whimsical whirl.

Cherries on top, they wink and sway,
As sprinkles dance in a colorful bay.
Spoons at the ready, we can't wait to dig,
In this frosty party, we all do a jig.

A Sundae's Sweet Serenade

With every scoop, a tale we tell,
Of creamy delights and a syrupy spell.
A scoop of laughter, a splash of cheer,
This sweet serenade will draw us near.

Chocolate rivers and vanilla clouds,
Echoes of joy, we sing out loud.
United in flavor, together we sway,
In this sundae symphony, we greet the day.

Colors of Joy in a Waffle Boat

In a crispy cradle, joy takes flight,
With every bite, the world feels right.
Strawberry waves and minty dreams,
Colors of laughter burst at the seams.

A sprinkle of fun, a touch of glee,
Waffle boat rides for you and me.
Scoops of happiness, piled up high,
Sailing on flavors, just you and I.

Drenched in Decadence

Beneath the drizzle of luscious charms,
Ice cream melts into sweet, warm arms.
Gooey delights splash over the side,
Drenched in decadence, we take the ride.

With every spoonful, the giggles flow,
Tasting happiness, we're all aglow.
Sundaes and smiles, a glorious team,
In this creamy wonder, we live the dream.

Nibbles of Summer Bliss

In the sun, we laugh and play,
With scoops of joy on a sunny day.
Flavors swirl, a creamy delight,
Each bite feels perfectly right.

Sprinkles dance like confetti here,
With each taste, we cheer and cheer.
A cherry on top, it's clear to see,
This bowl of dreams sets our hearts free.

Whirls of Happiness in a Dish

A duo of flavors, what a pair,
Swirling together without a care.
Crusty cones and laughter bold,
Rich tales of sweetness waiting to unfold.

Laughter rises with each spoon dive,
A creamy fantasy, we're alive!
Swirls of joy in colors bright,
This funny feast is pure delight.

Fruitful Fantasies from the Past

Chillin' with fruit, we reminisce,
Warm summer evenings, pure bliss.
Sticky fingers and silly grins,
Sipping laughter as the fun begins.

Every scoop, a story to tell,
Giggles mixed with a sweet caramel spell.
Old memories wrapped in a swirl,
A playful moment, let joy unfurl.

The Art of Indulgence

Crafted with joy, a colorful scene,
Layers of happiness, we keenly glean.
Spoonfuls of giggles, a swirl and a taste,
Every delightful bite, none go to waste.

Drizzled with mischief, a touch of flair,
Melting together, without a care.
We dance with flavor, let our hearts race,
In this tasty adventure, we find our place.

Rhythms of Richness and Cream

In a world of creamy delight,
Where scoops dance day and night,
Cherries bounce on top with flair,
Whipped cream clouds float in the air.

Sprinkles shower like falling stars,
While laughter echoes from candy bars,
Nuts rolling in a nutty spree,
All join in this tasty jubilee.

Cascades of Sweetness on My Palette

A river of fudge, oh what a sight,
Swirling happily, day or night,
Spoons clink as we share a laugh,
In this fruity, milky path.

Banana boats bob along the stream,
As we dip into our sweet dream,
Chocolate waves brush our toes,
In this dessert land, joy freely flows.

Adventures in Soft Serve

Twists and curls, a creamy ride,
A cone that giggles, can't be denied,
Sticky fingers from the fun,
Under the warm, glowing sun.

Toppings tumble like a wild theme,
Every bite bursts with a laughable beam,
Sprinkled giggles, peanut joy,
This soft serve's our favorite toy.

Twilight Tastes: The Delightful Mix

As day fades into a fruity swirl,
Candy corn twirls in a joyful whirl,
Sundaes glow under the moon's grin,
Where flavors dance and friendships begin.

Laughter bubbles in every bite,
Stars twinkle in the soft night light,
Chilled kisses of ice cream's gleam,
In this twilight, we all dream.

A Shimmer of Flavorful Enchantment

In a bowl of bright delight,
Scoops collide, what a sight!
Sprinkles tumble, colors gleam,
Dancing in a sugary dream.

Wobbly cherries, red so fine,
Thrive on ice cream, oh divine!
With each scoop, laughter blooms,
As toppings dance in joyful fumes.

Spoons twirl like playful sprites,
Underneath the summer lights.
Giggles echo, hearts engage,
In this creamy, sweet rampage!

Whispers of flavor wander near,
Promises of joy, sincere.
Life's a party, let's not quit,
With every bite, we're bound to split!

Medley of Memories on a Plate

A scoop of joy, a swirl of cheer,
Memories swirl with each yummy sphere.
Chocolate rivers flow so free,
In this playful, sweet jubilee.

The crunchy nuts sprinkle down,
As smiles bloom, not a frown.
Floating sprinkles on the top,
With each bite, we'll never stop.

Ice cream giggles as we cheer,
Fruity friends, all brought near.
Every spoonful tells a tale,
Of laughter and cheering, we can't fail.

Oh, what fun, let's celebrate,
With flavors bright, we'll not be late.
Every scoop a precious bond,
In this dessert-filled dreamy pond!

Poetic Pleasures of a Sweet Treat

A mountain high of frozen bliss,
Each creamy bite feels like a kiss.
Banana slices, oh, so bold,
Wrapped in dreams, a joy to hold.

Twinkling lights, a laughter spree,
As we serve a scoop of glee.
Whipped cream clouds on top so white,
With a cherry to light the night.

Nuts and sauces dance around,
Where happiness can always be found.
Grab a spoon, ignore the mess,
Let's indulge and feel the zest!

As flavors melt and mingle tight,
Joyful hearts take joyful flight.
In this world so rich and sweet,
Every treat feels like a feat!

Golden Echoes of Bananas Delight

In a sundae bowl, the echoes ring,
Of golden fruits and the joy they bring.
Scoops unite in a creamy whirl,
As laughter dances and flavors twirl.

Rainbow sprinkles on top do scatter,
In the coolness of sweet batter.
Cherry red, and smiles abound,
As we relive joy all around.

Ice cream rivers on the side,
Waves of laughter, let's take a ride.
Each bite a story, each dollop a dream,
Bursting with flavor, so light, so supreme.

Savor the moments, hear the cheer,
With frozen wonders drawing near.
In this lively, cheerful embrace,
A sweet delight, we joyfully chase!

Splashes of Summer on Cream

In a bowl of laughter we dive,
Scoops of joy help us thrive.
Bouncy cherries on top, oh so bright,
Creating smiles, pure delight.

Sunny rays in a swirl so sweet,
Crushed nuts dancing, a tasty treat.
Giggles escape with every bite,
Summer splashes, what a sight!

Whipped clouds floating all around,
Sugar-coated dreams abound.
With every drizzle, a cheerful cheer,
Life's simple pleasures drawing near.

So grab your spoon and take a chance,
Join the silly, sweetened dance.
With sprinkles of joy, we'll take the leap,
In this bowl of fun, we jump in deep.

Toppings of Tomorrow

Tomorrow's hopes piled up high,
A rainbow of dreams, oh my!
Chocolate rivers flow so wide,
Join the journey, take a ride.

Whipped dreams float on top, so light,
Coconut flakes drift in flight.
Sprinkles fall like confetti rains,
Pouring happiness through our veins.

Marshmallow clouds in a creamy sea,
Each scoop whispers, 'Come play with me!'
A fruity fiesta on every layer,
Building joy, a bold prayer.

With every flavor, laughter sings,
In this dessert, we find our wings.
Tomorrow's bliss in every bite,
Join the sweetness, feel the light!

Melodies in Every Layer

Layers of laughter softly blend,
Tuning hearts that never end.
A scoop of humor, a dash of fun,
Under the sun, we all run.

Fruity rhythms beat so fast,
Creating smiles that are meant to last.
Crispy crunch plays in the mix,
Join the melody, get your fix.

Each taste a note, a perfect rhyme,
Singing sweetly, just in time.
A chorus of flavors wrapped in cream,
Sprinkling joy, a perfect dream.

So let the sweetness fill your soul,
In every layer, we find our whole.
Come dance to this dessert's bright song,
In the laughter, we all belong.

A Slice of Golden Happiness

A slice of joy, oh what a treat,
Waves of laughter, can't be beat.
Golden ripe, the sun shines bright,
Fruity bliss in a happy bite.

Each spoonful brings a spark of glee,
Sharing smiles, just you and me.
Fudgy rivers fuse and flow,
Creating wonder in every show.

Scoops stacked high like dreams anew,
With every layer, we laugh and grew.
Swirls of magic twirl around,
Happiness in this world we've found.

So take a moment, feel the cheer,
In each sweet slice, love draws near.
With every taste, we find our bliss,
In this golden treat, a perfect kiss.

Sprinkles of Joy before the Dawn

In a bowl of bright delight,
Dancing with colors, oh so light.
Cherries vibrant on the top,
Sundae smiles never stop.

Spoon in hand, it's quite the quest,
Tasting laughter, feeling blessed.
Whipped cream clouds float through the air,
Sweetness giggles everywhere.

Morning mist with a fruity twist,
Dreaming flavors we can't resist.
Crunchy nuts make their bold appearance,
A sprinkle party, pure extravagance!

As laughter melts in every bite,
It's joy that makes the day feel bright.
So let's indulge without a care,
In this sundae land, nothing compares!

Nod to Nostalgia in Every Layer

A scoop of memory, creamy and sweet,
Waffle cones make the day complete.
Longing for summers, sun-kissed and bright,
Each layer whispers of pure delight.

Crispy edges, soft and warm,
Ice cream dreams take the storm.
As laughter echoes down the lane,
In every swirl, we feel the same.

Banana boats sail on a sea of cream,
Head in the clouds, we float and dream.
With sprinkles of joy, we make a toast,
To the flavors we cherish, and love the most!

Chocolate rivers flow, oh what a sight,
Diving in deep is pure delight.
With every bite, we find our bliss,
In a world where sweetness steals the kiss!

A Voyage of Taste and Imagination

Set sail on a sea of gooey delight,
Churning close to the golden light.
With every scoop, we journey far,
Riding waves beneath a candy star.

Whirlwinds of flavors, a magical ride,
Strawberry tides, with chocolate beside.
In hollers of joy, the flavors call,
As we plummet in sweetness, we eat it all!

Marshmallow fluff clouds in the sky,
Laughter takes wing, soaring high.
Every bite, a savory quest,
In this sundae ship, we are blessed.

Drifting on waves of creamy bliss,
Nostalgic taste, oh what a kiss!
Together we sail, no reason to stop,
In a bowl of dreams, we reach for the top!

Craving the Creamy Symphony

A symphony of flavors, a luscious tune,
Plays in our hearts like a sweet afternoon.
Bananas and berries in perfect blend,
With every scoop, the joys extend.

Melody flows with chocolate syrup streams,
Creating warm, delicious dreams.
We dip our spoons in creamy delight,
With giggles and crumbs, we own the night.

Orchestra of flavors, sweet and bold,
Every layer a story, waiting to be told.
Sprinkles like stars on this tasty cream,
Make every moment a playful dream!

So let the echoes of laughter ring,
In the symphony of joy that we bring.
With bowls of cheer and hearts that gleam,
We savor this life, living the dream!

Chilled Whispers of Delight

In a land where scoops collide,
Each flavor's a quirky guide.
Sprinkles dance in joyful flight,
Bananas giggle, warm and bright.

Chocolate rivers overflow,
Giggles ripple, sweet and slow.
Each bite a tiny, goofy grin,
Sundaes twirl, let the fun begin!

Marshmallow clouds above us sway,
With cherry cheers that come out to play.
Whipped cream mountains rise so tall,
In this land of sweet, we have a ball!

Cone hats tip, in silly cheer,
Laughter echoes, loud and clear.
Every flavor tells a tale,
In this dreamy snow-capped veil.

Frozen Fantasies in Sundae Splendor

Under the sunny sky's embrace,
A swirl of joy finds its place.
Toppings tumble, side by side,
A playful feast, let's take a ride!

Cherries laugh, as sprinkles fall,
In this dessert, we hear the call.
Marshmallow fluff bounces with glee,
Join the fun, come taste and see!

Scoops of wonder, piled so high,
Each cone a dream that flies on by.
The laughter spreads, like melting cream,
In each bite, there's sheer delight!

Waffle cones and sugar cones too,
Who knew dessert could be so true?
In this feast of frozen cheer,
Every spoon brings laughter near!

Creamy Reveries Beneath the Moon

Under the glowing starlit night,
A creamy wonder, pure delight.
With giggles soft, like whipped cream dreams,
Bananas chorus in moonlit beams.

Fudge rivers flow with silly grace,
Where marshmallows bounce, a playful race.
In this cold land, our hearts will play,
Each sundae here beckons to stay!

Scoops as high as wishes soar,
In every bite, there's room for more.
Drizzles dance with a frosty twirl,
In this creamy, dreamy swirl.

With laughter wrapping us like a hug,
Sundaes spark joy, that's the bug.
Let's savor whispers of the sweet,
And celebrate life with every treat!

A Symphony of Sweet Surprises

In a bowl, the magic swirls,
With giggles bright and twirling curls.
Every flavor sings a tune,
As we dive into this shared festoon.

Whipped cream mountains rise with flair,
While nutty notes drift through the air.
Salsa of sprinkles, oh so bright,
Dancing under the moonlight.

Chocolate dreams on a waffle bed,
With each little bite, joy spreads.
The fruit parade struts and beams,
In this frosty land of our dreams.

With laughter blending like sweet cream,
Each discovery, a brand new theme.
Join the symphony of delight,
As desserts ignite our playful night!

Medleys of Flavor in Twilight

In the twilight, flavors dance,
A scoop of laughter, take a chance.
Chocolate rivers, sugary skies,
Watching sprinkles as time flies.

Waffle boats on syrup seas,
Giggles swaying in the breeze.
Marshmallow fluff, a sweet surprise,
Oh, the joy in tasty pies.

Rainbow dreams with cherry tops,
Whipped cream towers, never stops.
Banana waves in sunset glow,
Belly laughs, the fun will flow.

Sundae songs in carefree flight,
With every scoop, a pure delight.
A medley spun in twilight's gleam,
Life's a bowl of endless cream.

A Journey Through Flavored Clouds

Let's float away on fudgey rays,
Through puffy clouds where candy plays.
Licorice vines hang from the blue,
A world where flavors come anew.

Popcorn sounds with each giggle,
As our silly spirits wiggle.
Honey drips from cotton candy,
Dreams are sweet and oh so dandy.

Lemon zest and vanilla spice,
Diving into the snow cone nice.
We bounce on marshmallow fluff,
In this journey, it's never tough.

Smoothie rain and berry trails,
Sailing through where laughter prevails.
With each scoop, the smiles grow,
In flavored clouds, the fun will flow.

Playful Scoops of Whimsy

A scoop of laughter, don't you know?
Banana slides in the sun's soft glow.
Chocolate chips like stars above,
Each bite bursts with joy and love.

Silly sprinkles, rainbow flair,
Tickling noses, delicious air.
Waffle cones fill up with grin,
In this world of fun we're in.

Laughter swirls in creamy streams,
Giggles mix with all our dreams.
Cotton candy sheep jump high,
Reaching flavors, oh my, oh my!

Whimsy sways on ice cream's breeze,
Together, it's a fun-filled tease.
Scoops that keep our spirits bright,
Playful scoops, pure delight.

Creamy Concoctions in Daydreams

In daydreams swirl the creamy blends,
Where giggly magic never ends.
Happiness served in sweet delight,
Each bite's a sprinkle of pure light.

Cherry moons on chocolate hills,
Banana peels bring silly thrills.
Marshmallow clouds serve joyful tunes,
Digging deep with playful spoons.

Sundaes stacked with dreams to share,
Laughter floats upon the air.
In this land of frosty cheer,
Creamy concoctions hold us near.

With every scoop a giggle blooms,
As flavors dance in our cozy rooms.
A tapestry of joy reveals,
What sweet concoctions dare to feel.

Dreaming in a Frosted Bowl

In the realm of creamy delight,
A scoop of laughter takes its flight.
Sprinkles dance like tiny stars,
While cherries wave from candy cars.

Wobbling easier than a clown,
The whipped cream smiles without a frown.
Nuts and fruit join in the cheer,
As giggles float like jelly, dear.

Every layer tells a tale,
Of flavors bold, they never pale.
With a spoon, we navigate,
This frosty bowl, a dream so great.

In this bowl, we laugh and play,
A silly feast in bright array.
With each bite, the world seems sweet,
In frosted joy, our hearts repeat.

The Art of Sweet Assembly

Crafting joy with every scoop,
A symphony of flavors in a loop.
Joyful chaos, a sticky spree,
As nuts and fruits join in glee.

Layers stacked in silly styles,
Creating laughter, mile after mile.
With every swirl, a giggle leaks,
As we embrace these dessert peaks.

Syrup rivers flood the way,
While chocolate waterfalls play.
With sprinkles flying, it's quite the sight,
In this sweet chaos, all feels right.

So come and join the frosty fun,
As smiles grow like the warming sun.
In every bite, we find our cheer,
This sweet assembly, so sincere.

Swirls of Fate in a Dessert Haven

In a land where sweetness reigns,
Where laughter spills from sugary veins.
Every swirl a twist of fate,
In this dessert, we celebrate.

Creamy tides come rushing in,
As giggling friends begin to spin.
With every scoop, a story's spun,
Of giggles shared and syrup fun.

Crumbling cones, they tumble down,
As flavors twirl in joyful clown.
Sugar clouds float high above,
In this haven, we find our love.

Each bite a giggle, each scoop a grin,
Whisk away our cares, let the fun begin.
In this sweet swirl, we're all aglow,
In a dessert haven, our joys overflow.

Nectar of Joy Drizzled on Dreams

A drizzle of nectar on creamy skies,
Bringing smiles and shared goodbyes.
A splash of joy, a hint of glee,
As flavors mingle, wild and free.

Sundaes tall as castles rise,
With peppers of laughter in every guise.
Chasing dreams with every bite,
This is where the world feels right.

Ribbons of chocolate twinkle and gleam,
In frosty wonder, we dare to dream.
With every twirl, the fun ignites,
Creating memories on dessert nights.

Sipping sunshine through creamy straws,
In this sweet nectar, we find our cause.
With giggles bubbling like fizzy streams,
Our hearts are full, the future beams.

Layers of Laughter and Lushness

Scoops of laughter piled high,
With sprinkles raining from the sky.
Cherries wobble, giggle with glee,
In this frosty rendezvous so carefree.

Whipped cream clouds drift overhead,
Where dreams of sweetness are widely spread.
Cones of comedy waddle along,
Dancing to a cheeky song.

Chocolate rivers swirl and twist,
A vortex of flavors you can't resist.
Giggles echo in the dessert sea,
As jests and jellies bounce in pure glee.

Layers stack in jubilant cheer,
A parade of pleasure, all sincere.
The laughter rolls like frozen delight,
Creating joy throughout the night.

When Bananas Dance in Delirium

In pajamas, bananas sway,
Bouncing, giggling, in a fruity ballet.
They twirl and spin in zany glee,
While ice cream bowls cheer with a hearty spree.

With every hop, they slip and slide,
Cheddar cheese can't hide its pride.
Whipped cream whirlwinds swirl around,
Bananas trip and flip to the sound.

Jelly beans join in the fun,
Creating a ruckus under the sun.
Chocolate chips roll on the ground,
As everyone joins the laughter bound.

In a pot of joy, they stew and blend,
A kooky fest that won't soon end.
With every twist, a giggly cheer,
As bananas dance without a fear.

Confections of a Blissful Night

In the moonlight, dessert ignites,
Sugary dreams take eccentric flights.
A twisty path of chocolate fun,
Where confections sparkle, one by one.

Caramel rivers flow with praise,
Under candy trees in a sugary maze.
Donuts skate on minty streams,
While marshmallow clouds float with beams.

Sundaes sparkle with cheeky grins,
As frosty smiles remain within.
Frumps and fumbles swirl in delight,
Creating giggles throughout the night.

With frosting fights that never cease,
In this paradise of sweet release.
Dreams are served up with a spoon,
A whimsical fest beneath the moon.

The Joy of Perfect Balance

On a platter of laughter, joy is served,
With every scoop, our fun preserved.
Balancing flavors in a splendid show,
Each ingredient dances, giving a glow.

Bananas sway, a zany pair,
Hatering toppings without a care.
In every bite resides delight,
A heavenly treat that feels just right.

Nuts roll over like giggling pals,
While ice cream twirls in fruity salves.
A laugh erupts from every taste,
No crumb of sweetness goes to waste.

In this harmony of crispy and smooth,
We find the giggles, the quirks, the groove.
A canvas of flavors, a joyous spree,
With perfect balance, we're always free.

Feast of Memories in a Dish

In a bowl of sunshine and glee,
A slice of joy, oh can't you see?
With sprinkles dancing all around,
Each bite a laugh, sweet joy is found.

Cherries on top, a crown of red,
A creamy castle, where smiles are spread.
Whipped clouds sail, with spoons we play,
Each flavor whispers, 'Come out and stay!'

Nuts are beacons, crunch in the night,
As we feast under the kitchen light.
Laughter erupts with every taste,
In this merry mix, let's not waste!

So let's dive deep, let giggles flow,
In this creamy dream, let joy overflow.
For each shared scoop is a treasure to keep,
In the feast of memories, we smile and we leap.

The Quest for the Perfect Scoop

With spoons held high, we set our sights,
On flavors that dance and take to flights.
A journey begins with a sweetened cheer,
In this land of frosty dreams, we persevere.

Minty breezes and chocolate streams,
With every dive, we chase our dreams.
Banana boats and fudge galore,
Each delightful bite, we ask for more!

We sail through puddles of caramel syrup,
A race to the bottom in a magical cup.
Creamy whispers call us near,
As we scoop up joy, and dispense the fear.

From waffle cones to sprinkle skies,
Our taste buds tickle, oh what a prize!
In this quest, we find our fate,
With every scoop, we celebrate!

Whispers of Creamy Delight

In a world where candy clouds float,
A scoop of laughter in every note.
Bananas sway like laughter's song,
With every lick, we can't go wrong.

Whipped dreams drape the sugary treat,
As joyous giggles fill the seat.
Waffle wonders and peanuts fall,
In this creamy world, we have a ball!

Each flavor tells a story sweet,
Of playful times and happy feet.
Melodies of fudge melt away,
With every taste, a bright new day.

So gather 'round, let laughter rise,
In this frosty land, where happiness lies.
With whipped wonders and joy in sight,
We dance through whispers of creamy delight.

Skimming Through Sweetness

With every scoop, we skim the bliss,
Caught in a whirl of sugary kiss.
Spoonfuls of joy swirl in the air,
Untamed excitement, we'll happily share.

Bright colors shine in every hue,
A carnival of flavors, oh so true!
Strawberries winking, vanilla dreams,
Together we laugh in cream-filled streams.

Oh, the thrill of flavors combined,
In our ice cream wonderland, joy is blind.
Fudge rivers flow, nuts tumble down,
In this joyous journey, we'll never frown.

So here we are, skimming the treat,
Life's sweetest moments, oh how they greet!
Let's dive into sweetness, hand in hand,
In this grand adventure, life tastes so grand!

Echoes of Laughter in a Bowl

In a dish so wide and round,
Scoops of joy swirl all around.
Sprinkles dance like stars in night,
Creating giggles, pure delight.

Spoons dive in, all made of glee,
Creamy chaos, wild and free.
Chocolate rivers flow with cheer,
Echoes of laughter fill the sphere.

Whiskers twitch and noses nibble,
Wobbly jigs and playful giggles.
Bananas laugh, they split with flair,
Every bite's a joyful dare.

At the end, with bowls all clean,
Everyone shares the tasty scene.
Sweetness lingers, smiles beguile,
Echoes of laughter, all worthwhile!

Harmony in Hues of Happiness

In a bowl of bright delight,
Colors dance, oh what a sight!
Yellow sunshine winks and grins,
Harmony, where laughter begins.

Raspberry swirls and minty dreams,
Giggles bubble like sweet cream.
Childlike joy in every scoop,
Harmony makes the flavors loop.

Syrup rivers flow with cheer,
Every flavor shares a gear.
Tropical tastes take a ride,
In this symphony, we abide.

With friends gathered, spoons unite,
Laughter echoes, hearts take flight.
In a medley of dessert and fun,
Harmony shines, a tasty run!

Flavors That Dream in Color

A scoop of pink, a dash of blue,
Tasty dreams await for you.
Chocolate drizzles, a twist of zest,
Flavors mingle, feeling blessed.

Rainbow sprinkles fall like rain,
Each bite's laughter, none in vain.
Fruity hums and creamy sighs,
In every taste, joy multiplies.

Marshmallow clouds on top so fluff,
Sweetened giggles, never enough.
Each flavor tells a silly tale,
In this bowl, we set our sail.

When the dish is clean and bare,
Nostalgic whiffs still fill the air.
Flavors whisper, colors gleam,
In this bowl, we chase the dream!

Delightful Tales Beneath a Cherry

Underneath a plump red hat,
Sits a tale that's full of chat.
Creamy tales spin around the bowl,
Knocking on each happy soul.

A cherry smiles with fruity flair,
While sprinkles jump without a care.
Scoops of laughter, laughter shared,
In sweets, we find how much we dared.

Nuts and fudge take a silly dive,
In this dessert, we truly thrive.
Giggles tumble as spoons collide,
With every bite, our joy won't hide.

When the bowl is licked quite clean,
We share our tales, a playful scene.
Delightful stories swirl and twirl,
Beneath that cherry, joy unfurl!

A Festival of Frosted Fantasies

In a land where ice cream rains,
And sprinkles dance like tiny trains,
The laughter echoes, flavors swirl,
As scoops of joy in chaos twirl.

A cherry atop a mountain high,
Dreams of dessert that touch the sky,
With waffle cones like towers stand,
Creating sweets that are quite grand.

The chocolate river flows with glee,
While marshmallow clouds drift lazily,
Every bite bursts out in cheer,
In this land, delight's always near.

So gather 'round, all friends and mates,
For treats that shatter all the fates,
In frosted realms of silly dreams,
Life's a feast, or so it seems!

Harmony of Subtle Sweetness

Beneath the swirl of whipped delight,
Dreams flash like fireworks at night,
Cone hats tipped with sprightly flair,
Sugary rhythms fill the air.

A festival of flavors collide,
Marshmallow clouds, they gently slide,
With each delightful, gooey bite,
Laughter bounces, spirits ignite.

The caramel rivers twist and turn,
With crispy edges, flavors burn,
While jelly beans prance in a line,
Creating joy, oh so divine.

In this place where sweets unite,
Every moment feels so right,
A toast to fun, we all shall raise,
In harmony of sugary ways!

Reflecting on Layers of Joy

Like a dessert with layers tight,
Dreams stack up in morning light,
Whipped cream crown on top so bright,
In every scoop, pure sheer delight.

Peanut butter waves softly flow,
As fudge rivers start to glow,
Count the sprinkles, laugh and cheer,
With each bit, the joy is here.

Candy ribbons drift and sway,
In a playful, sweet ballet,
Each flavor tells a tale anew,
With every taste, our happiness grew.

So lift your spoons, it's time to feast,
On layers rich, our worries ceased,
In this rhythm, laughter's reign,
Reflecting joy, it's never plain!

Confectionary Carnival at Midnight

Under stars where cupcakes gleam,
We ride the waves of sugar's dream,
The carousel spins with bright delight,
In a carnival of flavor's flight.

Gummy bears bounce, twirl and sway,
In this whirling, frosty display,
Each delicious, blissful cheer,
Brings laughter that we long to hear.

Cotton candy clouds drift so high,
As licorice laces thread the sky,
With chocolate ducks that quack and dive,
In this night, our spirits thrive.

So let the sweet parade unfold,
With tales of laughter yet untold,
A carnival where joy's the aim,
In the night's sweet, frosted game!

Dancing Flavors in Creamy Harmony

A cherry on top, a wobble, a twist,
All flavors collide in a sweet, fruity mist.
With every cold scoop, a giggle sets free,
As sprinkles cascade in a joyful decree.

Bananas do boogie, while sauce does a slide,
Each bite is a jig, no need to hide!
In this creamy dance, laughter takes flight,
Come on, join the fun, all hearts feel light.

Moments of Delight Before Bed

As the sun sets low and the stars start to peek,
A bowl full of giggles is all that we seek.
Chocolate rivers and marshmallow fluff,
These sweet little moments are perfectly tough.

With spoons in our hands, we share silly tales,
Of trips to the moon and adventurous whales.
As laughter erupts, the day melts away,
In creamy delight, we'll dream 'til the day.

Tasting Happiness, One Scoop at a Time

One scoop of joy and a swirl of delight,
Each taste brings a chuckle that dances in light.
With flavors combined like friends in a line,
A joyful ensemble, all perfectly fine.

Strawberry giggles and chocolate dreams,
A carnival in a bowl, bursting at seams.
With every small bite, the fun does expand,
A tasting adventure, so splendid and grand.

Echoing Dreams of Creamy Indulgence

In a world where fun flavors all come to play,
A chorus of sweetness leads us on our way.
Beneath a bright moon, a lavish delight,
Creamy adventures color the night.

With every cool scoop, we giggle and sway,
Echoing laughter that's here to stay.
Life's silly moments in flavors divine,
In a frosty embrace, all hearts intertwine.

Whimsical Scents of Summer

In the sun, we dance and sway,
With scents of sweet to savor each day.
Laughter rings like a joyous chime,
As ice cream drips, oh what a crime!

Beneath the trees, we giggle and play,
In sticky hands, treats melt away.
With every bite, the colors swirl,
Who knew summer could be this twirl?

Glistening Joys in a Glass

A glass filled high with creamy delight,
Swirls of colors, a marvelous sight.
With sprinkles singing, and fudge doing flips,
Each spoon brings cheers and laughter from lips.

Cherries on top, wearing their crown,
Wiggling, jiggling, never a frown.
Oops! It spills, but who cares about that?
Time to scoop up, oh what of that splat!

The Magic of Toppings and Treats

With sprinkles galore, they dance on the cone,
Each flavor whispers, you're not alone.
Chocolate or banana, a never-ending quest,
In a world where sweetness is truly the best.

Waffle cones laugh as they wobble and sway,
In a crunchy embrace, they holler hooray!
A dollop of joy, a splash of delight,
Each mouthful a giggle, pure summer delight!

Frosty Dreams with a Cherry on Top

Frosty delights in a rainbow parade,
With laughter echoed, sweet memories made.
Cherries like suns shining bright and bold,
In dreams of yummy, stories unfold.

Through giggles we share, let's scoop and dive,
Into frosty realms where taste buds thrive.
A mishap or two, just adds to the fun,
Who knew delight could be served by the ton?

The Sweet Quest Beneath a Slice

In a land where scoops reside,
Fruits and cream take a wild ride.
Cherries giggle, nuts do tease,
Sprinkles dance on sugary breeze.

A cone-shaped caper, oh what fun,
Whipped dreams melt beneath the sun.
Bananas wear their finest suits,
While chocolate gets in line with fruits.

One wobbly waffle, what a sight,
Stumbling soft, they laugh at night.
A sweet adventure, bold and bright,
In this quest, it's pure delight!

So scoot along, join the affair,
In this dessert, there's love to share.
A spoonful of laughter on your lips,
A joyous tale in every sip!

Banter Between Frost and Fruit

Frosty whispers tease the pear,
While a berry blushes way up there.
A banana brags, its peel so slick,
But a scoop of ice cream plays the trick.

"Come join the fun!" says a bright cherry,
But frosty lips stay cool and merry.
"Let's mix it up," a sprout demands,
As whipped cream swirls with playful hands.

Together they chase, in swirl and twirl,
A frosty giggle, a fruity whirl.
In this bowl of banter and grace,
Frost and fruit share a happy space.

So let them play, don't hold them back,
In the shade of a sundae shack.
A zany crew, frosty and sweet,
In laughter and joy, we all retreat.

A Lullaby in Layers of Sweetness

Under a crescent moon that beams,
A lullaby flows with rich cream dreams.
Layers of joy, piled up high,
Fruit melodies dance in the sky.

Pineapple whispers tales so sweet,
A crumbling cone joins in with beat.
Each scoop a story, full of flair,
Chocolate drizzle, floating in air.

Sprinkled stars above you gleam,
In tangled whispers of an ice cream dream.
Nuts serenade with tunes so bright,
While marshmallow fluff wraps you tight.

As slumbers drift on frosty sighs,
In this sweet haven, laughter flies.
A night of sweetness, full and grand,
In layers of joy, take my hand.

Rainbows in a Dessert Dish

In a bowl where colors clash,
Rainbows twirl in a sugary splash.
Each scoop a treasure, bright and grand,
With fruity jewels at our command.

Giggling spoons dive in for fun,
Where flavors race, all on the run.
A cherry's cheer, a chocolate grin,
Tells the stories of where we've been.

Underneath the lollipop sky,
Whipped wonders make the taste buds fly.
A circus of sweetness, oh so bold,
In this dessert, magic unfolds.

With every bite, a joke's been cracked,
A sprinkle here, another stacked.
Rainbows burst in this delightful dish,
In the sweet gusts of a flavor wish!

Sweet Whispers in a Desert Oasis

In the sun, a scoop of cheer,
Chilled delight, come gather near.
Where flavors dance on sandy ground,
Laughter echoes all around.

Mango, vanilla, mix and swirl,
A peanut crunch, watch it twirl.
Under cactus, we share a laugh,
A spoonful of joy, a frozen path.

With whipped cream clouds floating high,
Maraschino sun in the sky.
Taste the mirth, a sweet retreat,
In this land of icy treat.

So raise your cups and give a cheer,
For every scoop brings love near.
In this oasis, dreams take flight,
With every bite, we feel delight.

Flavorful Journeys Under a Cherry Top

On roads of fudge, we drive with glee,
A scoop of joy waits just for me.
With sprinkles sparkling like the stars,
We'll dine with smiles under Mars.

Toasty nuts and chilly cream,
Adventure stirs in every dream.
Each joyful layer, a surprise,
With cherry crowns, we claim the skies.

From lemon drops to peanut swirl,
A sweet escapade, watch it unfurl.
On waffle boats through flavor streams,
Navigating through dessert dreams.

In this world where giggles reign,
A splash of joy, forget the pain.
Flavorful journeys never stop,
So raise a spoon and take a hop!

Cradled by Cream and Cravings

Amidst the scoops, we find our way,
Creamy whispers, come what may.
Chocolate rivers, a sugary spree,
In this world of bliss, just you and me.

Frozen sprinkles, a confetti blast,
Sweet indulgence, a spell we'll cast.
Colors merge in a creamy sea,
Cradled by cravings, wild and free.

With laughter echoing through the air,
Chocolate fudge drizzled here and there.
Each bite's a giggle, pure and bright,
In our dessert wonder, we take flight.

So join the feast, don't hesitate,
For sweet adventure comes with fate.
Cradled in joy, with smiles abound,
In tasty dreams, true magic's found.

Chasing Frosted Wishes

In a world of frosted cheer,
A sprinkle of fun, bring it near.
Chasing wishes on a waffle scene,
A world of laughter, sweet and serene.

With every scoop, our giggles grow,
Syrup rivers in a cheerful flow.
Chocolate clouds up in the air,
Whipped dreams sprinkled everywhere.

Let's race for joy with spoons in hand,
In creamy delight, we take a stand.
Adventurous bites lead to our fate,
Chasing dreams, we celebrate.

So gather 'round, let laughter ring,
Frosted wishes make our hearts sing.
In this dessert land, come take a peek,
For humor thrives where flavors peak.

Frozen Fantasies and Cherry Wishes

In a bowl of frosty delights,
Scoops of joy, oh what a sight!
Here come cherries, round and red,
Dancing on top, it's easy to spread.

Sprinkles rain like confetti bright,
On creamy peaks, a splendid height.
A fizzy laugh, a spoon in hand,
With every bite, we take a stand.

Sundae gods, come take a bow,
For sweet delights, we cheer right now!
A swirl of fun, my taste buds cheer,
As silly flavors appear near.

With laughter brewed in frozen wells,
We share our smiles, oh how it gels!
Together in this frosty gale,
Our bubble of joy, we cannot fail.

Indulgence Wrapped in a Confection

A scoop of mischief, a dollop of glee,
Wrapped in a waffle, come dine with me.
Chocolate rivers flow and sway,
Nutty nuggets are here to play.

Each layer laughing, a funny tease,
A taste of chaos, oh yes please!
Whipped cream mountains, tall and grand,
One silly bite and oh! We stand.

Joyous giggles in every bite,
Sugar sprinkles, oh what delight.
Champions of cheer, we're on a quest,
For the sweetest treat, it's truly the best!

In the league of fun, we take our role,
As dessert warriors, together we stroll.
A cacophony of sugar, laughter and more,
This confection's a door to enjoy galore!

A Symphony of Flavor and Fun

Choco-drops play on a fruity stage,
While crazy toppings scream, "Turn the page!"
Spoons clash like cymbals, a tuneful joke,
In this frosty parade, we happily poke.

Melodies swirl in a creamy dream,
Sundae whistle, what a theme!
Banana boats sail through rivers sweet,
Adventure awaits with every treat.

We're tangle-footed on delicious tunes,
Flying high with sugar balloons.
Laughter echoes, a harmonious cheer,
In this flavor fest, we hold dear.

So raise your cups, spread joy anew,
In this joyful feast, we always pursue.
With each tasty note, we're free to fly,
A symphony of fun, as treats pass by!

Waves of Whipped Whimsy

Floating on waves of fluffy delight,
Whipped cream clouds dance in the light.
Each dollop a giggle, so soft and sweet,
Surfing on flavors, a frosty treat.

Sprinkled joy cascades like rain,
Creating smiles, washing away pain.
With cherries bobbing, a fruity spree,
We ride the crest of dessert jubilee.

Laughter splashes, a frothy cheer,
As silly tastes pull us near.
Past the shores of boring blues,
We paddle through flavor, no time to lose!

So bring on the sundae, the sprinkles, the fun,
In this whipped-up world, we've only begun.
With each colorful wave our spirits lift,
In our whipped whimsy, we find our gift.

A Canvas of Cream and Sprinkles

In a bowl full of joy, colors collide,
Fruits piled high, with laughter as a guide.
Whipped cream clouds dance, oh what a sight,
A sugary whirlwind, pure delight.

Crispy nuts rain down, a crunchy surprise,
As chocolate rivers flow, licking the skies.
Each spoonful a giggle, each bite a cheer,
Joy in every flavor, let's eat without fear!

Scoops of the rainbow, a melody bright,
Cherries on top, they're ready for flight.
Smiles in the sprinkles, happiness swirls,
In this creamy canvas, let's share with the girls!

So gather your friends, this treat is divine,
In a feast of soft dreams, let our hearts twine.
With every last scoop, our laughter will ring,
In this playful bowl, let's dance and sing!

Whirlpools of Luscious Wonders

Dive into flavors, a splash of sweet fun,
Twirl in the whirlpool, let the joy run.
Bananas swim round in a milky sea,
Chasing sprinkles and laughter, just you and me.

Spoons dig deep, uncovering gold,
Each bite a treasure, so joyous, so bold.
Caramel rivers, sticky and fine,
Dare you to dive in? Oh, it's all mine!

Chocolate swirls meet a coconut curl,
We're twinkling like stars, in a sugary swirl.
Giggles erupt with each slippery bite,
In this lush wonderland, we dance through the night.

So take my hand, let's float and explore,
In this ocean of sweetness, we always want more.
With every taste, the world starts to glow,
Whirlpools of laughter, in a flavor show!

Serenade of Sugary Bliss

Oh, listen closely, a melody sweet,
A serenade played on flavors we eat.
With notes of banana, a tune so grand,
Let's scoop up the laughter, hand in hand.

The symphony swirls in a creamy embrace,
Strawberry strums with a delicate grace.
Each layer a chorus of delights yet untold,
In this musical medley, bold flavors unfold.

Nutty harmonies blend with bright cherries,
Shaking our spoons like delightful fairies.
Fudgy crescendos cause giggles to rise,
A whimsical concert beneath sugar skies.

We'll clap and we'll cheer for this sugary play,
With voices of joy that will never decay.
A song of pure bliss, echoing thick,
In the serenade of a sweet tooth's pick!

Inspiration in Every Flavored Bite

With each spoonful taken, dreams take their flight,
In colors and tastes, everything feels right.
Crafted with joy, a masterpiece rare,
A canvas of sweetness, with brilliance to share.

Gentle giggles rise with every creamy swirl,
As flavors collide, a joyous whirl.
Sprinkles rain down like confetti in air,
Cheering us on, with a sparkly flair!

Each layer a story, a taste-bud ballet,
Inventive delights lead us astray.
Chocolate chips dance in a caramel dream,
Inspiration ignites, oh what a theme!

So come join the feast, let worries take flight,
In each flavored bite, we find pure delight.
Together we'll laugh, under dessert's bright light,
With every sweet memory, we'll sparkle tonight!

Echoes of Laughter from Dessertland

In a land where sweets gleam bright,
Toppings dance in pure delight,
Cherries giggle, sprinkles sing,
Joy can be found in everything.

Waffles wear a syrup crown,
Jelly beans bounce up and down,
In this world of frosted cheer,
Laughter echoes far and near.

Gumdrops tumble, and candies race,
Whipped cream's a fluffy embrace,
Every bite a chuckle, a smile,
Banana boats glide for a while.

So come join the tasty spree,
Where sweetness flows like comedy,
In Dessertland, dreams collide,
With every scoop, we laugh and glide.

Parfait Wishes Unfolding

In glasses tall and colors bright,
Layers dance in pure delight,
Granola crunch with yogurt swirl,
Each bite makes the taste buds whirl.

Whimsical flavors, a rainbow's wish,
Caramel drizzles like a playful fish,
Strawberries waltz in whipped cream's flow,
Banana dreams, they steal the show!

Nutty bits join fruit's parade,
A happy fest, never to fade,
Each spoonful brings a laugh so wide,
In this parfait, joy won't hide.

So scoop up the smiles, enjoy the treat,
Where happiness and sweetness meet,
In desserts' embrace, let's all unite,
With parfait wishes shining bright.

Sweetly Swirled Adventures

Twisting cones, oh what a sight,
Colors swirl in pure delight,
Ice cream fables spun so high,
Every scoop, a giggling sigh.

Sprinkle trails lead to the next,
Flavor hunts leave us perplexed,
Chocolate rivers, minty lakes,
Laughter bubbles, wonder wakes.

Fudge drizzles like a chocolate rain,
In this world, we feel no pain,
Sticky fingers, joyous grins,
Where every twist and lick begins.

So join the trek, the swirls, the spins,
In dessert's embrace, life always wins,
With sweetly swirled adventures near,
Let giggles echo, have no fear!

Slices of Joy on a Silver Spoon

Slices of fruit, a tasty art,
Curved on silver, they steal the heart,
Melony smiles with citrus spritz,
Each bite gives a joyful blitz.

Spoons of laughter, tastes collide,
In every fork, fun must abide,
Pineapple yells, "I'm fruity king!"
Bananas slide, and giggles spring.

Chocolate glimmers, a treasure found,
Bright and creamy joy abound,
Every treat a story spun,
Slices of joy, oh what fun!

So gather 'round for the spoon parade,
With every taste, the laughter's made,
In dessert's realm, we'll never part,
With sweet slices shared from the heart.

Melting Moments of Joy

On a sunny day, I took a treat,
A tower of flavors, oh so sweet.
Syrup drizzles like a slippery path,
Every bite sparks joyful laughter and math.

Cherry on top, a hat of delight,
Melting away, oh what a sight!
The scoops slide down, like joyful slopes,
A frozen treat filled with sweet hopes.

Strawberries giggle, bananas cheer,
In this whimsical world, no room for fear.
A whipped cream fountain, pure bliss so bright,
Melting moments of joy take flight.

Sprinkles rain down, a colorful dance,
I dip my spoon and join the romance.
With every scoop, my giggle expands,
In a dream of dessert, where laughter stands.

Sundae Serenades Under Starlight

Under the moon, the sundae stars glow,
Singing sweet tunes, oh, what a show!
Chocolate rivers flow through the night,
Bananas singing, a wonderful sight.

A symphony swirls in each creamy bite,
Whipped cream clouds float, oh, pure delight.
With a crunch from nuts, it's a crunchy song,
In this frosty dream, I can't go wrong.

Scoops of laughter, each spoonful a cheer,
Sprinkling smiles far and near.
In this sundae serenade, I find my tune,
Dancing in flavors, beneath the moon.

Maraschino smiles and caramel streams,
In this tasty night, I chase my dreams.
Under starlight's gaze, the joy won't end,
Sundae delights, with laughter, I blend.

Splattered Colors of Confection

Splash of pink, a drizzle of gold,
In this colorful mix, stories are told.
A canvas of sweetness, painting my day,
With each little bite, let worries fade away.

Splatters of fudge collide with the cream,
A colorful chaos, like a wild dream.
Banana boats sail on rivers of treat,
Giggles explode with every sweet beat.

Crumbles and sprinkles, a party so loud,
Colors of confection, making me proud.
With laughter and joy, I uncover the fun,
In this sugary bliss, my heart starts to run.

Twirling through flavors, I'm lost in the mix,
Swirling my spoon, I'm up to some tricks.
Splattered delights and unexpected cheer,
In this carnival of sweetness, I'll persevere.

Dreams Drizzled in Caramel

Caramel rivers flowing so sweet,
In a world of dreams, I can't be beat.
The golden cascade, a sticky embrace,
Drizzled and joyous, a flavorful race.

With every scoop, a giggle ignites,
Flavors collide in sweet, wild fights.
Bananas and sprinkles hang on for the ride,
In this gooey dream, let's slide side by side.

Swirling, twirling through sugary fun,
Chasing these flavors, I giggle and run.
With laughter and cream, my worries unfurl,
In dreams drizzled rich, I dance and I twirl.

A plate of delights, a feast for the soul,
So many flavors, that's how I roll.
Bathed in caramel, oh what a theme,
In this playful world, we dance and we dream.

Fruit and Froth: A Sweet Encounter

A scoop of laughter, oh so bright,
Whipped cream clouds amid the night.
Bananas jive with chocolate flair,
In this frothy dream, without a care.

Sprinkles dancing, colors collide,
Every bite, a wacky ride.
Fruits on parade, a carnival treat,
Joy served up, oh what a feat!

Melted magic drips like rain,
Silly faces, sugar's to blame.
A cherry atop, quirky and bold,
This frothy fun, a sight to behold!

In the land of smiles, we gather round,
Laughter and sweetness in every sound.
A circus of flavors, oh what a scene,
In this scooped delight, we live the dream!

Cravings Evoked by Chilled Delights

Oh, the fridge sings a frosty tune,
A chilly thrill beneath the moon.
Slices of fruit, a carousel spun,
In this icy treat, we laugh and run.

Sugar splashes create a storm,
In bowls of magic, we find our form.
Fruits laughing on a creamy wave,
Each scoop, a treasure we all crave.

Dreamy drips and cone oaths,
Wacky flavors, oh how they boast!
A giggle erupts with each spoonful shared,
Chilled delights, oh how they're cared!

So come together, feel the vibe,
Chilled sweet wonders, let's inscribe.
With every lick and silly grin,
In this sweet land, let the fun begin!

Ribbons of Joy on a Melting Plate

On a plate, ribbons swirl around,
A colorful symphony, laughter abounds.
Soft ice cream cascades like a stream,
In this playful feast, we live the dream!

A drizzle here, a sprinkle there,
Joy drips sweetly without a care.
Fruity signals, brightly displayed,
In melting moments, our worries fade.

Spoons become swords in fruit-filled fights,
In every bite, pure delight ignites.
Juggling flavors, we stammer and spin,
For with this treat, we all win!

So come sit down, it's time to share,
Ribbons of joy float through the air.
With giggles and toppings, let's play the game,
In our silly world, we're all the same!

Slices of Sunshine in Every Scoop

A scoop of sunshine on a darkened day,
With fruity friends, we laugh and play.
Cones stacked high, a wobbly sight,
As we dive in, joy takes flight!

Golden slices, cheerful and bright,
Each spoonful chased with pure delight.
Juicy wonders create a buzz,
In this flavor realm, laughter was!

Cherry hats and cooling treats,
Every layer, a dance that beats.
With silly faces, we savor the fun,
Under the sun, we're never done!

So grab a scoop, let the giggles flow,
In this scoop-town, we steal the show.
Slices of sunshine in every bite,
In our happy hearts, everything feels right!

www.ingramcontent.com/pod-product-compliance
Lightning Source LLC
Chambersburg PA
CBHW062110280426
43661CB00086B/406